Eric Bray

New
Time
to
Communicate

NAN'UN-DO

New Time to Communicate
Copyright© 2015 by Eric Bray

音声ファイル
無料 DL
のご案内

このテキストの音声を無料で視聴（ストリーミング）・ダウンロードできます。自習用音声としてご活用ください。
以下のサイトにアクセスしてテキスト番号で検索してください。

https://nanun-do.com　テキスト番号 [**511699**]

※ 無線 LAN（WiFi）に接続してのご利用を推奨いたします。

※ 音声ダウンロードは Zip ファイルでの提供になります。
　お使いの機器によっては別途ソフトウェア（アプリケーション）の導入が必要となります。

※ New Time to Communicate 音声ダウンロードページは
以下の QR コードからもご利用になれます。

Table of Contents

Unit 1 *Meeting People* 7

Unit 2 *Getting to Know Your Classmates* 11

Unit 3 *Talking About Classes* 15

Unit 4 *Talking About Your Daily Life* 19
Review and Reflection Units 1-4

Unit 5 *Talking About People - Personality* 24

Unit 6 *Talking About People - Appearance* 29

Unit 7 *Talking About Last Weekend* 34

Unit 8 *Talking About the Vacation* 39

Unit 9 *Talking About Going Out on the Town* 43
Review and Reflection Units 5-9

Unit 10 *Talking About Foods and Recipes* 49

Unit 11 *Talking About Travel* 53

Unit 12 *Talking About Hometowns* 57

Unit 13 *Talking About Your Opinions* 61

Unit 14 *Talking About Future Plans* 65
Review and Reflection Units 10-14

Unit 15 *Review and Practice* 70

Extra Activities 74

Message to Students

Welcome to the New Time to Communicate! Five units and many new activities have been added to this textbook, but its purpose remains the same: to help students improve their abilities to communicate in English. The conversations you will practice are the kinds of conversations you might have when speaking with people from other countries, either here in your country or when traveling abroad. The activities and exercises are all designed to help you learn the vocabulary, grammar and common expressions you need to have these conversations and to have fun doing so! And so, without further ado...it's Time to Communicate!

New
Time
to
Communicate

Unit 1
Meeting People

1) Model Conversation — Introducing Yourself

Task 1 Two students meet at a welcome party for new students. Practice the conversation with a partner.

A: Hi, I'm Jun.

B: Nice to meet you. I'm Akiko.

A: Nice to meet you. Where are you from?

B: I'm from Tokyo. How about you?

A: I'm from Osaka.

　　What part of Tokyo are you from?

B: I grew up in Setagaya-ku.

Follow-Up Question

Task 2 The conversation continues. Practice with a partner.

A: I see. What do you like to do in your free time?

B: Sorry, could you repeat that, please?

A: Sure. What do you like to do in your free time? You know... Do you have a hobby?

B: Well, I like to watch movies a lot. I also like listening to music.

A: Oh, really? What kind of music do you like? ◀········ **Follow-Up Question**

B: I really like J-Pop, and sometimes I listen to classical music.

> **Follow-Up Questions**
> Follow-up questions are used when the speaker has told you something and you want more information.

- 7 -

2) Useful Language 1 — How Should You Address Your Teacher?

Task *Look at these ways of addressing your teacher. Decide if they are Good (commonly used), Maybe OK, or Not OK (unnatural or rude). Mark each one using the correct code. The first one has been done for you.*

Good = ○
Maybe OK = ?
Not OK = ×

Example

In a greeting with
the author's name
 Eric   Bray
(first name) (family name)

_×_ Hi, Eric Bray.
____ Hi, Bray.
____ Hi, Eric.
____ Hi, Mr. Eric Bray.
____ Hi, Bray teacher.
____ Hi, Bray sensei.
____ Hi. Eric teacher.
____ Hi, Eric sensei.
____ Hi, Mr. Eric.
____ Hi, Mr. Bray.

3) Useful Language 2 — Words and Expressions You will Hear

Task *Look at the words and expressions on the left, and write the letter in the blank of the definition on the right that best matches it. The first one has been done for you.*

Expressions you will hear

1. follow-up question _g_
2. homework ____
3. guess ____
4. make a group ____
5. practice with a partner ____
6. repeat after me ____
7. compare your answers with a neighbor ____

Definitions

a. join together with 2 or 3 people
b. do the conversation with another person in class
c. check your answers with the person next to you
d. give an answer when you are not sure
e. say what the teacher says after he/she says it
f. work you do at home
g. a question you ask when you want more information

4) Conversation Activity — Meet Your Class Members

Task *Walk around the classroom and introduce yourself to your class members. Write down their names and some information about what they like to do in their free time.*

Example

A) Hi, my name's Kazuo.
B) Nice to meet you. My name's Hiro.
A) What do you like to do in your free time?
B) I like to watch movies at home.   **Follow-Up Question**
A) Oh, really? What movie do you like a lot?
B) I really like the last Lord of the Rings movie.
A) Yeah. That's a good movie.

Free time Activities

watch movies	play the piano
read books	listen to music
talk with friends	go shopping
use the computer	cook food
play TV games	play soccer
_____	_____

Class member's name	...do in your free time?
Hiromi	watch movies

5) Listening — About Yourself

Task *Listen to the following passage. Write the words you hear in the blanks.*

I'll tell you a bit about myself. My name is 1_____.

I'm from 2_____ , and I grew up in 3_____.

In my free time I like to 4_____ . I also like 5_____.

My dream for the future is 6_____.

6) Write and Talk — About Yourself

Task *Write about yourself. You can use the passage above as a model. When you finish, close the book and talk about yourself with a partner or small group.*

Unit 2
Getting to Know Your Classmates

1) Model Conversation — What's Your Major?

Task 1 Two students meet again. Practice the conversation with a partner.

A: Hi. We met last week. You're Akiko, right?
B: That's right. I remember you. You're Jun.
A: Yeah, I didn't ask you. What's your major?
B: Major? What does "major" mean?
A: Your major is the main subject you study.
   It's your department in the university.
B: OK, then I'm an Economics major.
A: Oh, really. I study in the Law department.

Common Subject Names			
Economics	経済学	Law	法　学
Sociology	社会学	Psychology	心理学
English	英語学	Engineering	工　学
Japanese Literature	日本文学	Business	経営学
Science and Technology	理工学	_____	_____

Task 2 The conversation continues. Practice with a partner. Notice the follow-up questions.

B: I see. What year are you?
A: I'm a third year student.
B: A third year student... Right...
   <u>Do you</u> live alone or with your family? ◄········ **Follow-Up Question**
A: I live with my family. How about you?
B: I'm a first year student. I live alone now.
A: I see. <u>Where</u> do you live? ◄········ **Follow-Up Question**
B: I live in an apartment near the train station.

- 11 -

2) Useful Language — Follow-Up Questions

Task 1 *The words and phrases in this Follow-Up Question Starter Box will help you write good follow-up questions. Translate the contents into Japanese.*

Follow-Up Question Starters

What...?	Who...?	How...?
When...?	Why...?	Where...?
Which...?	Whose...?	Are you...?
Can you...?	Do you...?	Did you...?
How long...?	How much...?	How many...?
How often do you...?	Have you ever...?	

What? ____なに____   Who? _____   How? _____
When? _____   Why? _____   Where? _____
Which? _____   Whose? _____   Are you? _____
Can you? _____   Do you? _____   Did you? _____
How long? _____   How much? _____   How many? _____
How often do you? _____   Have you ever? _____

Task 2 *Imagine that someone says these things to you in a conversation. Write good follow-up questions in the blank spaces.*

Example 1. A) I saw a good movie last night.
       B) What movie did you see?
       B) Where did you see it?   ◄········ Follow-Up Questions
       B) Did you see the movie with a friend?
       B) How often do you see a movie?

2. A) I really like cooking.
    B) What can you _____?
    B) How often do you _____?

3. A) I went shopping at Daimaru yesterday.
    B) What did you _____?
    B) Who did you _____?

4. A) I woke up very early this morning.
    B) Why _____?
    B) What time _____?

5. A) I really like my part-time job.
    B) _____?

6. A) I want to go to Europe next year.
    B) _____?

3) Conversation Activity — Find Out About a Classmate

Task 1 *Read the questions below and then write two questions of your own. Then sit across from your partner and introduce yourself. Next, take turns asking each other the questions. Use the Follow-Up Question Starter Box to help you ask follow-up questions. Take notes on your partner's answers.*

Example

A) Hi, I'm _____.

B) Nice to meet you.

    My name is _____.

A) Where are you from?

B) I'm from _____.

Follow-Up Question Starters

What...?	Who...?	How...?
When...?	Why...?	Where...?
Which...?	Whose...?	Are you...?
Can you...?	Do you...?	Did you...?
How long...?	How much...?	How many...?
How often do you...?		Have you ever...?

Interview Questions	Partner's Answers (notes)	Follow-Up Question Answers (notes)
Where are you from?		
Where do you live now?		
Do you have any brothers or sisters?		
What's your major?		
What do you like to do in your free time?		
Do you have a part-time job?		
What's your favorite TV show?		
What food do you like a lot?		
Who's your favorite singer or musical group?		
What did you do during the last vacation?		
What's your dream for the future?		
Your question...		

Task 2 *Join another pair of students and tell them about your partner using the notes you have written. Introduce your partner by saying:*

Hi, this is _____. She's/He's from _____.

4) Listening — Learning More About Others

Task *Listen to the following passage. Write the words you hear in the blanks.*

I'll tell you a little bit more about myself. I live in 1_____ now. I'm a 2_____ . My favorite foods are 3_____ and 4_____ . My major is 5_____ . My favorite musical group is 6_____ . I really want to see their concert someday.

5) Write and Talk — More About Yourself

Task *Write about yourself. You can use the passage above as a model. When you finish, close the book and talk about yourself with a partner or small group.*

_____
_____
_____
_____
_____
_____
_____
_____
_____
_____
_____
_____

Unit 3
Talking About Classes

1) Model Conversation — Talking About Classes

Task 1 *Two friends talk at school. Practice the conversation.*

A: Hi. How's everything going?

B: Pretty well. I'm taking some good classes this term.

A: Oh yeah? What's your favorite class so far?

B: I like my Computer class a lot. It's really interesting.
We learn how to use different software in class. How about you?
What's your favorite class?

A: Hmmm... I have a great Sociology class, but there's a lot of reading.

B: Yeah, I know what you mean. I took a Sociology class last year.

Task 2 *The conversation continues. Write in the missing questions and then practice with a partner.*

A: What's your hardest class?

B: I'm taking Spanish 1 this term. It's really difficult.

A: *Why*_____? ◄········ **Follow-Up Question**

B: It's difficult because the grammar is really complicated.

A: Yeah, but the pronunciation is simple. For example, do you know
the Spanish word "casa"? You just say — CA-SA. It's easy to say, right?

B: Yeah, you're right.
By the way, *what*_____? ◄········ **Follow-Up Question**

A: "Casa" means house in Spanish.

B: Wow, you know a lot. I may have some questions about Spanish for you this year.

- 15 -

2) Useful Language — Expressions for Conversation Management

Task *Put numbers in the blanks to match the expressions on the right with the situations on the left. The first one has been done for you.*

Situations   Expressions

You don't understand what someone says.
____1____

You don't understand the meaning of a word someone uses.
_____

You don't know how to spell an English word.
_____

You don't know how to pronounce an English word.
_____

You know the Japanese word, but you don't know the English word for it.
_____

1. Could you repeat that please?

2. What does (English word) mean?

3. How do you pronounce this (English word)?

4. What's the spelling of (English word)?

5. What's the word for (Japanese word) in English?

6. Could you say that one more time, please?

7. How do you spell (English word)?

8. How do you say this word (English word)?

9. What's the meaning of (English word)?

10. Could you speak more slowly, please?

11. How do you say (Japanese word) in English?

3) Conversation Activity — Find Someone Who...

Task Look at the question topics under "Find Someone Who..." and write questions in the blanks. Also, make up one Yes/No question of your own. Go around the class and ask your classmates the questions. When someone answers "Yes," write their name in the blank. Be sure to ask follow-up questions, and write that information in the blank too.

Follow-Up Question Starters

What...?	Who...?	How...?
When...?	Why...?	Where...?
Which...?	Whose...?	Are you...?
Can you...?	Do you...?	Did you...?
How long...?	How much...?	How many...?
How often do you...?	Have you ever...?	

Find Someone Who...	Question	Name	Follow-Up Question Answers
is from Kobe			
saw a movie last month			
has an older sister			
likes to cook			
was born in October			
can play a musical instrument			
has a part-time job in a restaurant			
went shopping last weekend			
has a pet			
woke up today before 6 a.m.			
lives alone			
has traveled abroad			
your question...			

Unit 3 *Talking About Classes*

4) Listening — Learning About Someone's Classes

Task *Listen to the following passage. Write the words you hear in the blanks.*

I'll tell you about my classes this term. This term I'm taking 1_____ classes per week. Last term I had more classes, so my schedule is 2_____.

So far my favorite class is 3_____. It's really interesting.

My hardest class is 4_____. My most difficult day is 5_____. It's difficult because 6_____.

5) Write and Talk — About Your Classes

Task *Write about yourself. You can use the passage above as a model. When you finish, close the book and talk about your classes with a partner or small group.*

_____
_____
_____
_____
_____
_____
_____
_____
_____
_____
_____

Unit 4

Talking About Your Daily Life

1) Model Conversation — What's Your Typical Day Like?

Task 1 Two friends talk at school about their schedules. Practice this conversation with a partner.

A: Hi, how's it going?

B: Pretty good. How about you?

A: OK. But I've got a new schedule, so I'm pretty busy.

B: Oh really? What's your typical day like?

A: Well, I usually get up at 6:00. I eat breakfast and leave the house by 7:00. I often stay at school until 4:30 or so, and then go back home. At home I eat dinner, and study a bit. Then, sometimes I watch TV before going to bed.

B: That doesn't sound so busy.

A: Yeah, but the university is a long way from my home.

Task 2 The conversation continues. Write in the missing questions and then practice with a partner.

B: I see... *Where* _____ ? ◀······· Follow-Up Question

A: I live outside of Nagoya. My home is in the countryside.

B: Oh, really?

A: Yeah, it takes me almost 2 hours to come to school.

B: Really... *How* _____ ? ◀······· Follow-Up Question

A: I come to school by bus and train. How about you?

B: I'm lucky. I can come to school by bicycle. It only takes about 15 minutes.

Follow-Up Question Starters		
What…?	Who…?	How…?
When…?	Why…?	Where…?
Which…?	Whose…?	Are you…?
Can you…?	Do you…?	Did you…?
How long…?	How much…?	How many…?
How often do you…?	Have you ever…?	

- 19 -

2) Useful Language — Back-Channeling (Aizuchi)

Task 1 In a natural conversation the listener often uses back-channeling (Aizuchi) to show the speaker that he/she is listening and understands the speaker. Here are some examples of expressions used to back-channel in English. Write some expressions you use to back-channel in Japanese in the box on the right.

English		Japanese
Um...	Uh-huh...	
Right...	Yeah...	
Really...	I see...	
OK...	Hmmm...	

Task 2 Look at the conversation below and fill in the blanks with back-channeling expressions from the box above.

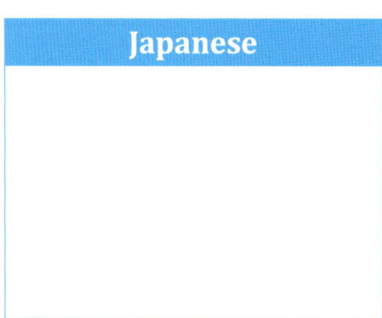

A) It's a nice day today.

B) _____.

A) I might go for a drive.

B) _____.

A) Hey... Do you want to go with me?

B) _____. Let me look at my schedule.....
I'm pretty busy. I need to study for a test tomorrow in Chemistry.

A) _____.

B) But I could go for a couple of hours.

A) Great! Let's get ready.

Task 3 First, practice the conversation above with a partner. Then, use the Write and Talk Assignments you did in Units 1, 2 and 3 to tell your partner about yourself. Pause after some of the sentences so your partner can practice back-channeling.

3) Conversation Activity — How Often Do You...?

Task *Guess how often your partner does the activities listed on the chart below. Mark your guess with an ○. Write a question of your own. Then ask your partner about the activities and mark the answers you hear with a check ✓. Practice back-channeling when your partner answers and use the follow-up question box on page 19 to help you ask follow-up questions. Write the answers you hear in the blanks.*

Example

A) How often do you wake up before 7 a.m.?
B) I always wake up before 7 a.m.
A) I see. What time do you usually go to bed?
B) About 11:30 p.m.

Follow-Up Question

Frequency Adverbs
always - 100%
usually - 70%-90%
often - 40%-90%
sometimes - 10%-40%
hardly ever - 5%-10%
never - 0%

How often do you...?	always	usually	often	sometimes	hardly ever	never	Follow-up answer
wake up before 7 a.m.							
have toast for breakfast							
skip breakfast							
get to school late							
eat lunch in the cafeteria							
take a nap in the afternoon							
eat dinner with your family							
watch TV at night							
go to bed before 11 p.m.							
go to bed after 2 a.m.							
sleep in on Sunday							
study on the weekend							
your question							

When you finish: How many times did you guess correctly? _____

Unit 4 — Talking About Your Daily Life

4) Listening — About a Typical Day

Task *Listen to the following passage. Write the words you hear in the blanks.*

I'll tell you about my typical day. I usually wake up 1_____.

I always 2_____ before breakfast.

For breakfast I 3_____. I often leave the house at

 4_____ and stay at school until 5_____.

In the evening I 6_____.

5) Write and Talk — About Your Typical Day

Task *Write about yourself. You can use the passage above as a model. When you finish, close the book and talk about your typical day with a partner or small group.*

Review and Reflection — Units 1-4

Task *Use the questions below to help you review and reflect on what you have studied in the last four units.*

1. What new words, expressions, or grammar patterns did you learn and think are important to remember?

   _____
   _____
   _____
   _____
   _____

2. Write sentences using these new words, expressions or grammar patterns.

   _____
   _____
   _____
   _____
   _____
   _____
   _____

3. What else did you learn about language, culture or language learning?

   _____
   _____
   _____
   _____
   _____

Unit 5
Talking About People - Personality

1) Model Conversation — Tell Me About Your Family

Task 1   Two friends talk about people in their families. Practice this conversation with a partner.

A: Hi. What's new?

B: Not much. I had dinner with my family last night.

A: Oh, really? Can you tell me about your family?

B: Sure. There are six people in my family - My mother, my father, my big brother, my younger sister, my grandmother and me. How about you?

A: Wow, that's a big family! There are four people in my family, me, my brother, my mom and my dad.

B: I see. What's your dad like?

A: He's very smart. He has a lot of hobbies. He really enjoys his life.

B: Hmmm. My dad's kind of shy, but he's really funny sometimes.

Task 2   The conversation continues. Write in the missing questions and then practice with a partner.

B: How about your brother? _____? ◄········ **Follow-Up Question**

A: He's a nice guy. He's pretty easy-going.

B: I see. What does he like to do in his free time?

A: He's really into playing computer games.

B: Oh, really? _____? ◄········ **Follow-Up Question**

A: Recently he likes to play Grand Theft Auto and Street Fighter. Sometimes he stays up until late at night playing games.

B: Yeah, I have a friend who loves Street Fighter.

Follow-Up Question Starters		
What...?	Who...?	How...?
When...?	Why...?	Where...?
Which...?	Whose...?	Are you...?
Can you...?	Do you...?	Did you...?
How long...?	How much...?	How many...?
How often do you...?	Have you ever...?	

- 24 -

2) Useful Language 1 — Character Adjectives

Task The words on the left are used to describe a person's character or personality. Put the number of the word in the blank next to the definition on the right that best matches it. The first one has been done for you.

1. easygoing
2. funny
3. talkative
4. nervous
5. friendly
6. smart
7. serious
8. selfish
9. moody
10. quiet
11. stubborn
12. independent
13. impatient
14. shy
15. thoughtful

a. ____ makes people laugh
b. ____ intelligent, thinks clearly
c. ____ doesn't talk very much
d. ____ feelings change often; emotional ups and downs
e. ____ doesn't like to wait
f. ____ happy to do things alone
g. ____ only cares about him/herself, not others
h. ____ not flexible, wants to do things his/her own way
i. ____ makes friends easily
j. _1_ relaxed, takes things as they come
k. ____ works hard, does not play around
l. ____ kind, thinks of other people's feelings a lot
m. ____ not relaxed, does not feel calm
n. ____ talks a lot
o. ____ not outgoing, doesn't meet new people easily

3) Useful Language 2 — Degree Adverbs

Task Degree adverbs are used to strengthen/weaken an adjective. We often use degree adverbs to make speech more polite. Look at the examples of how degree adverbs are used, and then write some sentences using degree adverbs about friends, family members or famous people you know.

-	+	++	+++
not very	kind of	fairly	very
not so	a bit	pretty	really

Examples

1) My older brother is kind of impatient.
2) My friend Bob is really moody.
3) Tamori is pretty funny.

1. _____
2. _____
3. _____
4. _____
5. _____

Unit 5 Talking About People - Personality

- 25 -

4) Conversation Activity — Information Gap

Task *Ask your partner questions like those in the Model Conversation below. Then write the information in the blanks in the chart.*

Student A

Model Conversation

1) A) Where's <u>Hitomi</u> from?
   B) <u>She's</u> from <u>Tokyo</u>.
2) A) Where does <u>she</u> live now?
   B) She lives in <u>Nagoya</u>.
3) A) What does <u>she</u> do?
   B) She's a <u>university student</u>.
4) A) What does <u>she</u> like to do in her free time?
   B) <u>She</u> likes to <u>read books</u>.
5) A) What time does <u>she</u> usually wake up?
   B) <u>She</u> usually wakes up at <u>6:30</u>.
6) A) What's <u>she</u> like?
   B) She's very <u>easygoing</u>.

	1	2	3	4	5	6
Name	Hometown	Live Now	Do (Work)	Free Time	Wake Up	Character
Hitomi	Tokyo	Nagoya	university student	read books	6:30	very easygoing
John		Kyoto	English teacher		8:30	
Kenji		Yokohama/ family	high school student			kind of quiet
Taka	Nagoya		college student	study English		
Beth		Kobe			6:00	pretty independent
Michiko	Kyoto			meet her friends		very talkative
(Your Partner) ____						

- 26 -

4) Conversation Activity — Information Gap

Task *Ask your partner questions like those in the Model Conversation below. Then write the information in the blanks in the chart.*

Model Conversation

1) A) Where's <u>Hitomi</u> from?
   B) <u>She's</u> from <u>Tokyo</u>.
2) A) Where does <u>she</u> live now?
   B) She lives in <u>Nagoya</u>.
3) A) What does <u>she</u> do?
   B) She's a <u>university student</u>.
4) A) What does <u>she</u> like to do in her free time?
   B) <u>She</u> likes to <u>read books</u>.
5) A) What time does <u>she</u> usually wake up?
   B) <u>She</u> usually wakes up at <u>6:30</u>.
6) A) What's <u>she</u> like?
   B) She's very <u>easygoing</u>.

Student B

	1	2	3	4	5	6
Name	Hometown	Live Now	Do (Work)	Free Time	Wake Up	Character
Hitomi	Tokyo	Nagoya	university student	read books	6:30	very easygoing
John	San Francisco			take a long walk		really thoughtful
Kenji	Yokohama			play computer games	7:00	
Taka		New York/ girlfriend			9:00	a bit stubborn
Beth	London		works/trading company	do pottery		
Michiko		Osaka/ husband	works/at home		7:15	
(Your Partner) _____						

Unit 5 Talking About People - Personality

- 27 -

5) Listening — People in Your Life

Task *Listen to the following passage. Write the words you hear in the blanks.*

I'll tell you about some people in my life. My mom is a great person. She is

1_____. She often 2_____.

I met my best friend Dave in high school, and we get along really well.

He's 3_____. We usually 4_____

_____. I get along with almost everybody, but I don't

really like people who are 5_____ or 6_____.

6) Write and Talk — People in Your Life

Task *Write about yourself. You can use the passage above as a model. When you finish, close the book and talk about people in your life with a partner or small group.*

_____
_____
_____
_____
_____
_____
_____
_____
_____
_____
_____
_____

Unit 6
Talking About People - Appearance

1) Model Conversation — What Does He Look Like?

Task 1 *Two young women talk about a friend. Practice this conversation with a partner.*

A: Hi, Junko... My friend John is coming to visit this weekend. Would you like to meet him?

B: Sure, what's he like?

A: Well, he's friendly but sometimes he's a bit stubborn. I've known him since my high school days.

B: Oh, I see... What does he look like?

A: Well, he's tall and his hair is kind of long. He's fairly handsome. I think you'd like him.

B: OK, he sounds nice.

Task 2 *The conversation continues. Write in the missing questions and then practice with a partner.*

B: By the way, what are John's hobbies?

A: Well, he plays the guitar and he's in a band with some friends. They're going to play in a club here this Saturday.

B: Oh, really? _____? ◀······· **Follow-Up Question**

A: They play rock music...and some blues too. I've seen them play a couple of times. It was a lot of fun. Do you want to go see them with me?

B: Sure, I'd love to! _____? ◀······· **Follow-Up Question**

A: The show starts at 9 p.m.

B: Great. Let's go together.

A: OK... I'll introduce you to John on Saturday.

Follow-Up Question Starters		
What...?	Who...?	How...?
When...?	Why...?	Where...?
Which...?	Whose...?	Are you...?
Can you...?	Do you...?	Did you...?
How long...?	How much...?	How many...?
How often do you...?	Have you ever...?	

- 29 -

2) Useful Language — Describing Appearance

Task *Here are some words used to describe what people look like (appearance). Listen and practice the questions and descriptions.*

1. What's his/her face like?

Example - His/Her face is kind of round.

round   oval   thin   triangular   square

2. What's her/his hair like? **Color**

Example - Her/His hair is straight and black. black, dark brown, light brown,
(length before color) blonde, red, gray

straight   wavy   curly   short   shoulder length

long   parted on the side   pulled back   (She has) bangs   (He is) bald(ing)

3. What are his/her eyes like? **Color**

Example - He/She has big brown eyes. black, brown, blue, green, hazel
(size before color)

big   small   narrow   almond-shaped

4. What are her/his eyebrows like?

Example - She/He has rather thin eyebrows.

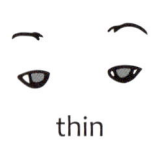 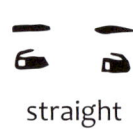  

thin   straight   arched   bushy

- 30 -

5. What's his/her nose like?

Example - His/Her nose is a bit large.

large   flat   turned-up   broad   small

6. What's her/his mouth like?

Example - She/He has thin lips.

thin lips 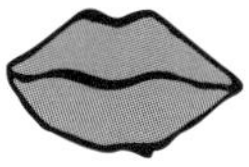   full lips    a big smile    a small smile

7. What else can you tell me about his/her face?

Example - He/She has a light complexion.

a light/dark complexion   a beard   a mustache   (wears) glasses

8. How is she/he built?

Example - She's/He's short and kind of thin.

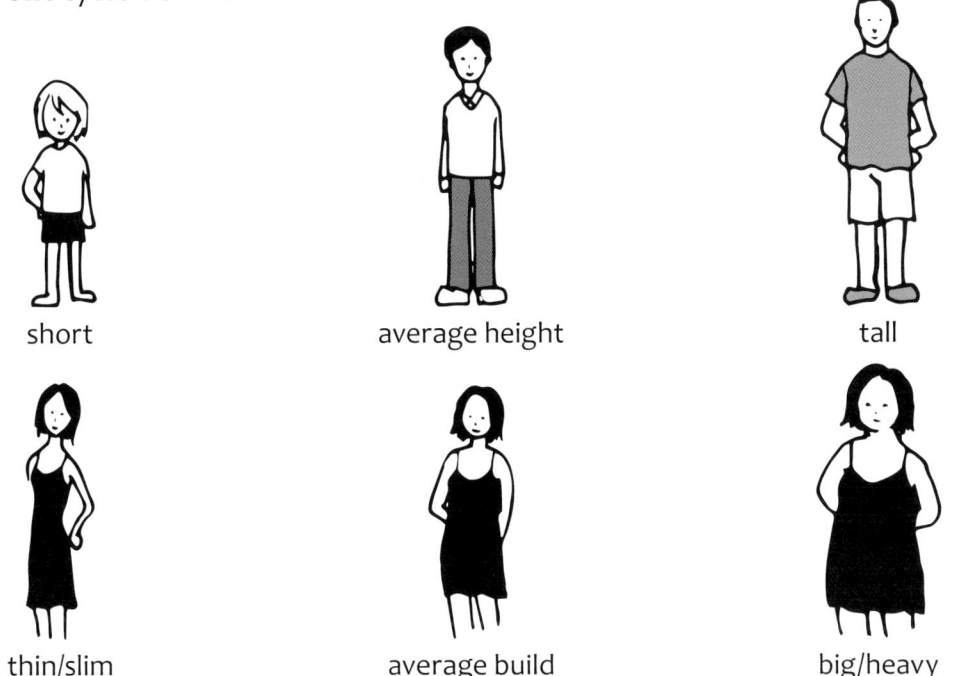

short   average height   tall

thin/slim   average build   big/heavy

3) Conversation Activity — Draw the Face and Guess Who it is

Task *Ask your partner the questions you just practiced in the Useful Language section about a photo of a famous person. As you listen, draw a picture of the face of the person your partner describes. Guess who the person is, and write the name of the person in the blank. Ask for a hint if necessary. Ask these two questions first:*

1. Is this person a man or a woman?
2. What country is this person from?

1. Name _____

2. Name _____

3. Name _____

4. Name _____

4) Listening — People in Your Life

Task Listen to the following passage. Write the words you hear in the blanks.

I'll tell you more about some important people in my life. Alex is a good friend of mine. We met at my part-time job last year. He's 1_____ and 2_____. Another friend is Melissa. She has 3_____ and 4_____. We met in high school. My oldest friend is Steve. We met in elementary school. He's 5_____ and 6_____.

I'm lucky to have such good friends.

5) Write and Talk — People in Your Life

Task Write about yourself. You can use the passage above as a model. When you finish, close the book and talk about people in your life with a partner or small group.

Unit 7

Talking About Last Weekend

1) Model Conversation — How Was Your Weekend?

Task 1 Two young women talk about the weekend. Practice this conversation with a partner.

A: Hi, how was your weekend?

B: Great! On Saturday I worked at my part-time job in the afternoon.
   Then I met my boyfriend for dinner. We went to an "all you can eat" Italian buffet.
   The food was tasty and cheap, too.

A: That sounds good. How about Sunday?

B: I went shopping with a friend.

A: Did you buy anything?

B: No, I was just "window shopping." But my friend bought a nice jacket.
   We found a cake shop, drank some tea and talked a long time.

A: That sounds like a good weekend!

Task 2 The conversation continues. Write in the missing questions and then practice with a partner.

B: How about you? How was your weekend?

A: It was pretty good. On Saturday I cleaned my room. On Sunday
   I went out for lunch with my older sister.

B: How was that?

A: Well, we had a good chat. But she was kind of tired.

B: _____? ◄········ **Follow-Up Question**

A: She went out dancing the night before with some friends.

B: _____? ◄········ **Follow-Up Question**

A: They went to a club called World. After that they went to sing karaoke until morning.

B: Wow, your sister really knows how to have a good time!

Follow-Up Question Starters		
What...?	Who...?	How...?
When...?	Why...?	Where...?
Which...?	Whose...?	Are you...?
Can you...?	Do you...?	Did you...?
How long...?	How much...?	How many...?
How often do you...?	Have you ever...?	

- 34 -

2) Useful Language — Past Tense Verb Forms

Task 1 This list contains the 25 most common verbs used in English, plus a few more you will find useful. Write the past tense forms of these verbs in the space on the right. Notice that some of the verbs are regular verbs that end in "ed," and others are irregular verbs.

Verb Base Form	Past Tense Form	Verb Base Form	Past Tense Form
listen	*listened*	buy	
go	*went*	look	
talk		clean	
is		watch	
do		relax	
eat		make	
play		have	
sleep		ask	
want		work	
tell		meet	
cook		study	
see		sing	
stay up late		take a nap	
run into		get dressed	
chat with		wait for	

Task 2 Think about your week. Complete the sentences below using the past tense verbs above.

Example - Last Friday I bought a new guitar.

1. Last Saturday _____
2. Yesterday morning _____
3. Yesterday afternoon _____
4. Last night _____
5. This morning _____
6. Before this class _____

- 35 -

3) Conversation Activity — Information Gap - Last Weekend

Task *Ask your partner questions like those in the Model Conversation below. Then write the information in the blanks in the chart.*

Model Conversation

Student A

1) A) What did Hitomi do <u>last Saturday</u>?
   B) <u>She saw a movie</u>.
2) A) Who did she go with?
   B) <u>She went with some friends</u>.
3) A) How was it?
   B) It was <u>pretty good</u>.
4) A) How much did she spend?
   B) She spent <u>about 2,000 yen</u>.
5) A) How often does she <u>see a movie</u>?
   B) <u>She sees a movie about once a month</u>.
6) A) What did she do on Sunday?
   B) <u>She went driving with a friend</u>.

Name	1 Do Saturday?	2 Who...with?	3 How was it?	4 How much?	5 How often?	6 Do Sunday?
Hitomi	saw a movie	some friends	pretty good	2,000 yen	about once a month	went driving
Joe		his girlfriend			twice a year	studied at home
Shin	played golf			5,000 yen	once a month	
Hiro		alone		3,500 yen	every night	
Kris	went out to eat	her husband				visited parents
Maiko	relaxed at home		not bad		most Saturdays	
(Your Partner) _____						

3) Conversation Activity — Information Gap - Last Weekend

Task: Ask your partner questions like those in the Model Conversation below. Then write the information in the blanks in the chart.

Model Conversation — Student B

1) A) What did Hitomi do <u>last Saturday</u>?
   B) <u>She saw a movie</u>.

2) A) Who did she go with?
   B) <u>She went with some friends</u>.

3) A) How was it?
   B) It was <u>pretty good</u>.

4) A) How much did she spend?
   B) She spent <u>about 2,000 yen</u>.

5) A) How often does she <u>see a movie</u>?
   B) <u>She sees a movie about once a month</u>.

6) A) What did she do on Sunday?
   B) <u>She went driving with a friend</u>.

Name	1 Do Saturday?	2 Who...with?	3 How was it?	4 How much?	5 How often?	6 Do Sunday?
Hitomi	saw a movie	some friends	pretty good	2,000 yen	about once a month	went driving
Joe	went to a concert		so so	5,000 yen		
Shin		his brother	really good			cleaned the house
Hiro	went to the pub		OK			slept in late
Kris			a lot of fun	65 dollars	every weekend	
Maiko		her cat		0		practiced bass guitar
(Your Partner)						

4) Listening — Last Weekend

Task Listen to the following passage. Write the words you hear in the blanks.

I'll tell you about my weekend. On Friday night 1_____.

That was a lot of fun. On Saturday morning I woke up and 2_____.

On Saturday afternoon 3_____. Then on Saturday night some

friends and I 4_____. I got home really late. It was

an expensive evening. I spent 5_____. On Sunday

6_____. All in all it was a good weekend.

5) Write and Talk — About Last Weekend

Task Write about yourself. You can use the passage above as a model. When you finish, close the book and talk about last weekend with a partner or small group.

Unit 8

Talking About the Vacation

1) Model Conversation — How Was Your Vacation?

Task 1 *Two friends talk after the vacation. Practice this conversation with a partner.* 🔘 28

A: Hi, long time no see.

B: Yeah. How was your vacation?

A: It was great! I went to Yakushima. It's an island near Kyushu.

B: Oh really? Who did you go with?

A: I went with a friend from my high school days.

B: That sounds fun. What did you do there?

A: We swam a lot and did some hiking too. We saw this big tree called "Jomon Sugi." It's more than 2,000 years old. Have you heard of it?

B: Yeah. I want to see it some day.

🔘 29

Task 2 *The conversation continues. Write in the missing questions and then practice with a partner.*

A: How about you? How was your vacation?

B: It was good. I got my driver's license.

A: Really? _____? ◄········ **Follow-Up Question**

B: It took about a month. But it was kind of expensive.

A: Oh, really? _____? ◄········ **Follow-Up Question**

B: It cost about 200,000 yen. I paid half myself.

A: Good for you! Let's go driving some day.

B: Sure, anytime.

Follow-Up Question Starters		
What…?	Who…?	How…?
When…?	Why…?	Where…?
Which…?	Whose…?	Are you…?
Can you…?	Do you…?	Did you…?
How long…?	How much…?	How many…?
How often do you…?	Have you ever…?	

2) Useful Language — Common Mistakes to Avoid

Task *This task introduces some conversational expressions commonly used to talk about vacation activities. Look at the pairs of sentences below. One is not standard English. Circle the correct sentence in each pair.*

1. I went to abroad.   or   I went abroad.

2. I went to the beach.   or   I went to sea.

3. I saved much money.   or   I saved a lot of money.

4. I took my driver's license.   or   I got my driver's license.

5. I worked as a tutor.   or   I worked as a home teacher.

6. I went to shopping.   or   I went shopping.

7. I took a trip in Japan.   or   I took a travel in Japan.

8. I backed to my hometown.   or   I went back to my hometown.

9. I played with my friends from high school.   or   I got together with my friends from high school.

10. I went to a party with my club seniors.   or   I went to a party with my older club members.

11. I hope I can go to Okinawa again.   or   I wish I can go to Okinawa again.

12. I was surprising that the vacation went by so fast.   or   I was surprised that the vacation went by so fast.

3) Conversation Activity — Find Someone Who...

Task Look at the question topics under "Find Someone Who..." and write the questions in the blanks. Also make up a Yes/No question of your own. Go around the class and ask your classmates the questions. When someone answers "Yes," write their name in the blank. Be sure to ask follow-up questions, and write that information in the blank on the right.

Find Someone who...	Question	Name	Follow-Up Question Answers
had a part-time job			
traveled abroad			
swam in the ocean			
got a driver's license			
went to a concert			
saw a movie in a theater			
attended a club training camp			
went shopping with a parent			
quit a job			
went fishing			
visited a grandparent's house			
met a new boyfriend or girlfriend			
read a lot of comics (manga)			
your question...			

Unit 8 *Talking About the Vacation*

4) Listening — About the Vacation

Task *Listen to the following passage. Write the words you hear in the blanks.*

I'll tell you about my vacation. 1_____.

That was a lot of fun. Every day 2_____.

Some days 3_____.

At night 4_____.

One night 5_____. The only bad thing that

happened was that 6_____. Other than that,

it was a great vacation.

5) Write and Talk — About Your Vacation

Task *Write about yourself. You can use the passage above as a model. When you finish, close the book and talk about your vacation with a partner or small group.*

Unit 9
Talking About Going Out on the Town

1) Model Conversation — Making Plans for the Weekend

Task 1 *Two friends talk about the weekend. Practice this conversation with a partner.* 31

A: Hey, are you busy this weekend?

B: No, I don't think so. Why?

A: Do you want to see a movie? There's a new Batman movie at the theater downtown I want to see.

B: That sounds good. I love all the Batman movies.

A: OK. How about Friday night? We can meet at the Starbucks in front of the train station at 7 p.m. Then we can walk to the movie theater from there.

B: OK, Let me check my schedule... Oh, that's too bad. I forgot I have to work at my part-time job on Friday night.

A: No problem. Let's go another night.

Task 2 *The conversation continues. Write in the missing questions and then practice with a partner.* 32

A: How about getting together on Saturday night? Do you have any plans?

B: No, I'm free on Saturday. How about seeing that Batman movie?

A: Sure. But maybe we could eat dinner first and then see the late show.

B: Good idea. _____? ◄········ **Follow-Up Question**

A: Let's meet in front of the big clock at the train station. I know a good Thai restaurant near there.

B: OK. _____? ◄········ **Follow-Up Question**

A: Shall we meet at 6? That will give us plenty of time to eat.

B: Great! That sounds like a good plan. I'm looking forward to it!

Follow-Up Question Starters		
What...?	Who...?	How...?
When...?	Why...?	Where...?
Which...?	Whose...?	Are you...?
Can you...?	Do you...?	Did you...?
How long...?	How much...?	How many...?
How often do you...?	Have you ever...?	

2) Useful Language — Location Expressions

Task 1 Read the sentences that describe the location of the places on the map. Find the places on the map, and write the number of the place in the square. The first one has been done for you.

1. Starbucks is in front of the train station.
2. The post office is next to the train station.
3. The bank is down the street from the train station.
4. The movie theater is behind the train station.
5. The Softbank shop is diagonally across from the train station.

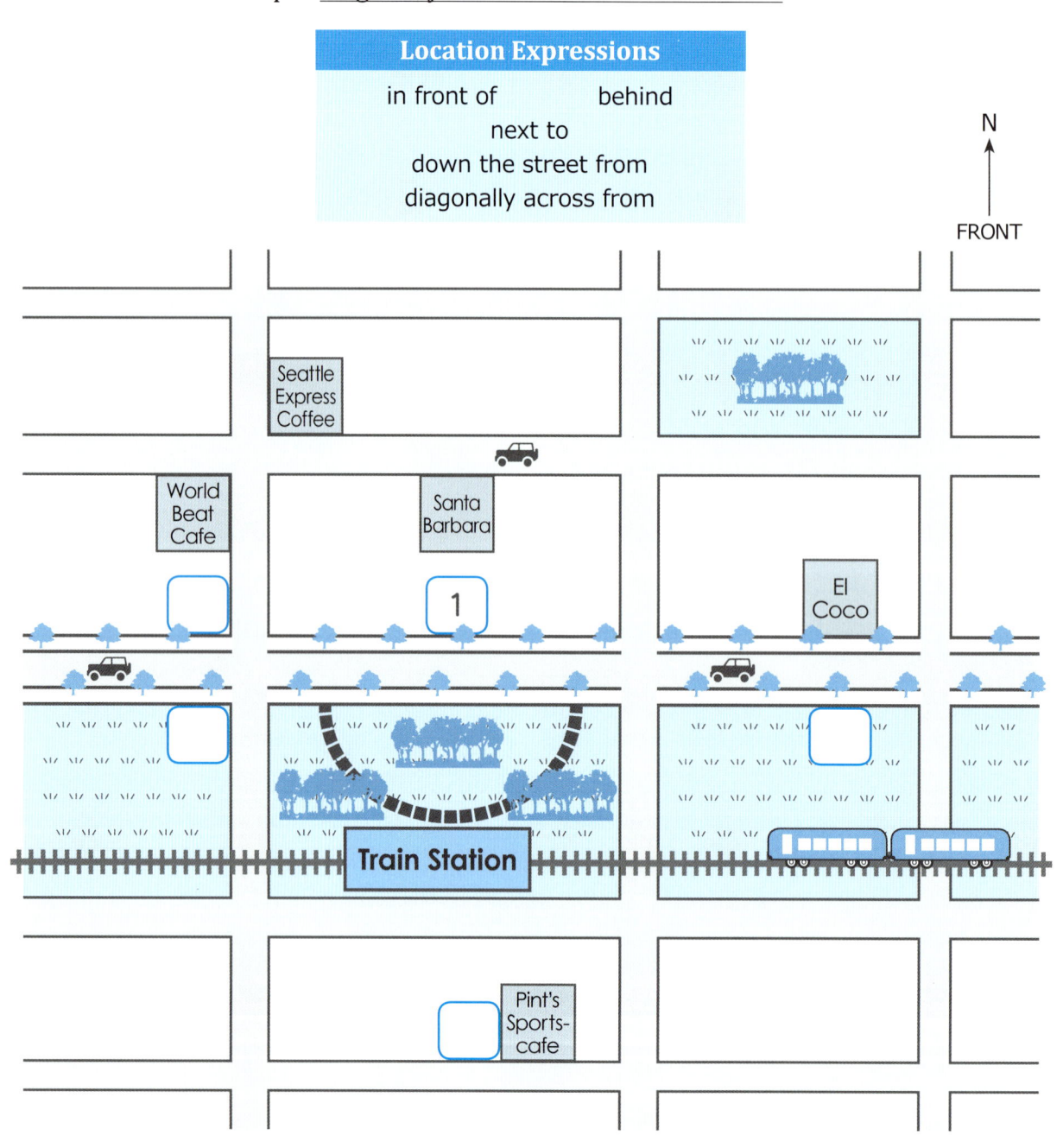

Location Expressions

in front of   behind
next to
down the street from
diagonally across from

Task 2 *Find these places on the map. Write a sentence to describe their location. The first one has been done for you.*

1. The World Beat Cafe *is down the street from the Santa Barbara.*
2. Pint's Sportscafe _____
3. El Coco _____
4. Seattle Express Coffee Company _____
5. The Santa Barbara _____

3) Conversation Activity — Accepting and Refusing Invitations

Task *Pretend you have the next week off from school and want to go out every night. Invite your classmates to join you.*

1. Look at the ads on page 45 and decide which place you want to go to. Choose a day you want to go, and write the place and what you want to do there on the calendar.

2. Decide on a time to meet. Look at the map on page 44, and decide what would be a good meeting place. Write this information on the calendar.

3. Choose one day you are busy because of your part-time job. Write "part-time job" in this space on the calendar.

Model Conversation

A) Would you like to go to <u>El Coco for a drink</u>?

B) That sounds like fun. When are you going?

A) <u>Friday night at 7:00</u>.

(accept)	(refuse)
B) Sure, I'm free Friday. Where shall we meet?	B) Sorry, I'm busy on Friday night.
	or
A) Let's meet in front of the train station.	Sorry, I have to work on Friday night.
B) Great. See you there at 7.	A) OK. No problem. Let's meet another time.

< Weekly Calendar >

Day	Place/Activity	Meeting Time	Meeting Place
Monday			
Tuesday			
Wednesday			
Thursday			
Friday			
Saturday			
Sunday			

4) Listening — A Night Out on the Town

Task *Listen to the following passage. Write the words you hear in the blanks.*

I'll tell you my plans for a fun night out on the town. Let's meet at the coffee shop 1_____. From there we can walk to the new cafe 2_____. They have an interesting menu and the food is really tasty. From there we can 3_____. They have live music on Friday nights. We should 4_____. The trains run 5_____. But if you want to go home by taxi, we can 6_____. Does that sound like fun?

5) Write and Talk — Your Night Out on the Town

Task *Write about yourself. You can use the passage above as a model. When you finish, close the book and talk about your plan with a partner or small group.*

- 47 -

Review and Reflection — Units 5-9

Task *Use the questions below to help you review and reflect on what you have studied in the last five units.*

1. What new words, expressions, or grammar patterns did you learn and think are important to remember?

   _____
   _____
   _____
   _____
   _____

2. Write sentences using these new words, expressions or grammar patterns.

   _____
   _____
   _____
   _____
   _____
   _____
   _____

3. What else did you learn about language, culture or language learning?

   _____
   _____
   _____
   _____

Unit 10
Talking About Foods and Recipes

1) Model Conversation — That Sounds Delicious!

Task 1 *Two students talk in the cafeteria. Practice this conversation with a partner.* 35

A: Hi... Do you mind if I sit here?

B: No, go ahead, have a seat.

A: Thanks. Do you eat in the cafeteria often?

B: No, I usually bring a box lunch. But my mom is visiting her relatives, so I'm eating in the cafeteria today.

A: I see. So your mom cooks for you every day. You're lucky. I live alone so I have to cook for myself.

B: Oh, you know how to cook. That's great. What dishes can you cook?

A: Well, I can cook dishes like Fried Rice and Chicken Curry.

Task 2 *The conversation continues. Write in the missing question and then practice with a partner.* 36

A: How about you? _____? ◄······· **Follow-Up Question**

B: Sure, I can cook a little bit. My mom is teaching me how to cook some simple dishes.

A: Can you tell me the recipe for a dish you can cook?

B: OK, this is a dish I learned recently. I'll tell you the recipe.
The ingredients are: pasta, milk, olive oil, onion, bacon, salt, black pepper and egg.
The directions are:
First, you boil water and put in the pasta. Drain the pasta when it's cooked.
Next, you chop up the bacon and onion and fry them in oil.
Then, you add milk, salt, black pepper and some egg.
Finally, pour the sauce over the pasta and mix well. Then it's ready to eat!

A: That sounds delicious!

B: Can you guess what this dish is called?

A: Hmmm... Is it Scrambled Eggs?

B: No, it isn't.

A: Is it _____?

B: You're right!

2) Useful Language 1 — Cooking Words

Task Write the words from the box into the correct blanks.   37

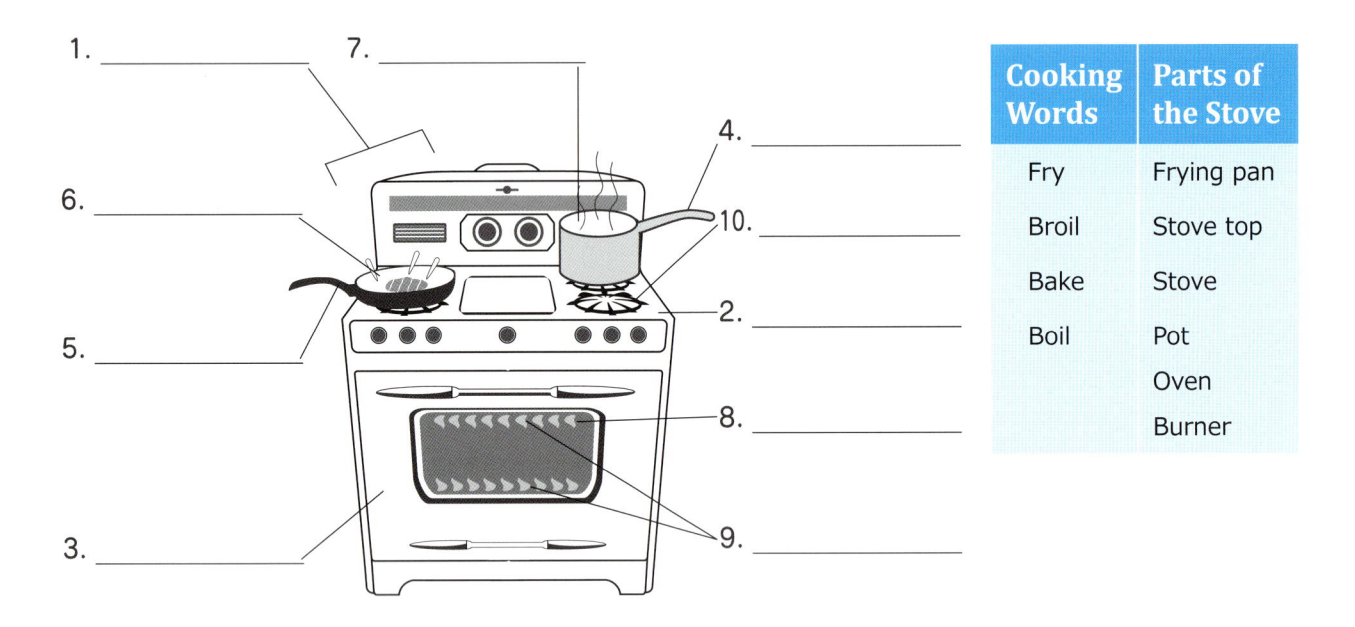

1. _____
7. _____
4. _____
6. _____
10. _____
2. _____
5. _____
8. _____
3. _____
9. _____

Cooking Words	Parts of the Stove
Fry	Frying pan
Broil	Stove top
Bake	Stove
Boil	Pot
	Oven
	Burner

3) Useful Language 2 — Foods and Cooking Words

Task Here are some foods and some more cooking words. Listen to a recipe for a delicious dish. As you listen the first time, circle the ingredients you hear mentioned. As you listen the second time, circle the directions you hear. Can you guess the name of the dish?

The dish is _____   38

Foods - Ingredients

egg	black pepper	milk	soy sauce	herbs	sugar	salt
bell pepper	spinach	bread	cheese	oil	eggplant	pork
wine	cucumber	noodles	mushroom	radish	green onions
fish	carrot	broth	vinegar	beef	shrimp	flour
potato	bread crumbs	banana	beans	chicken	onion

Cooking words - Directions

break	put in	chop up	cut up	mix up	wash
sprinkle	pour in	steam	add	heat up	taste
take out	turn on	grate	peel	barbeque	fold	mash
stirfry	turn over	cook	turn off	scramble	microwave

- 50 -

4) Conversation Activity — Can You Guess This Dish's Name?

Task 1 *In the spaces below, list the ingredients and write out the directions for making a dish or snack you like. Be sure to use, "First...," "Next...," "Then..." and "Finally..." when you write your directions. Use the conversation on page 49 as your model.*

Your Recipe

Ingredients:	Directions
1.	*First, you...*
2.	
3.	
4.	
5.	
6.	
7.	
8.	
9.	
10.	

Task 2 *Now tell your recipe to your group. Have them try to guess the name of your dish. Write the names of the dishes in your group in the blanks.*

Dishes in your group: _____ _____

_____ _____

5) Listening — About Foods and Dishes You Like

Task *Listen to the following passage. Write the words you hear in the blanks.*

I'll tell you about my favorite foods. I like vegetables a lot. I especially like

1_____. I love fruits too, and try to eat some every day.

My favorite fruits are 2_____. I eat a lot of fish, and

I 3_____. I could 4_____.

My favorite dishes are 5_____.

But I don't like 6_____.

6) Write and Talk — About Foods and Dishes You Like

Task *Write about yourself. You can use the passage above as a model. When you finish, close the book and talk about foods and dishes you like with a partner or small group.*

_____
_____
_____
_____
_____
_____
_____
_____
_____
_____
_____

Unit 11

Talking About Travel

1) Model Conversation — Have You Ever Been to...?

Task 1 *Two university students talk in Kyoto. Practice this conversation with a partner.* 🎧 40

A: Hi, I'm Chen. Nice to meet you.

B: I'm Kenji. Where are you from, Chen?

A: I'm from China. I'm a foreign student here.

B: Oh, I see. How long have you been in Japan?

A: I've lived in Japan for five years. I started university in Kyoto three years ago.

B: How do you like Kyoto?

A: It's great! I like the mountains and the temples. Yesterday I hiked up Daimonji Mountain. I could see all of Kyoto. It was a great view. Have you ever hiked up Daimonji?

B: No, I've never done that. But I've always wanted to.

Task 2 *The conversation continues. Write in the missing questions and then practice with a partner.* 🎧 41

B: Have you traveled to any other places in Japan?

A: Yeah. I went to Sapporo last Spring. I did some skiing and snowboarding. It was a lot of fun. Have you ever tried skiing or snowboarding?

B: Yeah, in fact, I'm in the ski club at my university. We haven't taken any long trips yet, but we have gone to Nagano a few times.

A: _____? ◀······· **Follow-Up Question**

B: It's really nice. The mountains are beautiful. It's not so far from Kyoto.

A: _____? ◀······· **Follow-Up Question**

B: We went by night bus. It's cheaper than going by car or train.

A: I can't sleep on night buses, but it sounds like fun.

Follow-Up Question Starters

What...?	Who...?	How...?
When...?	Why...?	Where...?
Which...?	Whose...?	Are you...?
Can you...?	Do you...?	Did you...?
How long...?	How much...?	How many...?
How often do you...?	Have you ever...?	

- 53 -

2) Useful Language — Present Perfect

The Present Perfect is used to talk about things that: 1) happened in the past when the exact time is not important or 2) happened in the past and continue in the present.

Examples

Have you ever traveled abroad?

I have traveled abroad three times in my life.

He has known her for ten years.

Task 1 *The verb form used in the Present Perfect is have + past participle. The regular past participle form is the same as the regular past form (base form + "ed") But some past particle forms are irregular. Fill in the blanks with the correct verb forms.*

Verb base Form	Past	Past Participle Form	Verb Base Form	Past	Past Participle Form
travel	*traveled*	*traveled*	drink		
know	*knew*	*known*	come		
give			fly		
like			see		
sing			do		
eat			drive		
take			bring		
begin			swim		
choose			wear		
become			go		
feel			use		
write			try		
is			think		
hear of			call up		
wake up			get together with		

Task 2 *Read the sentences and circle the correct verb form.*

1. I (played/have played) the guitar for ten years now.
2. So far I (visited/have visited) Korea five times.
3. I (ate/have eaten) noodles three times yesterday.
4. Have you ever (swam/swum) in the sea?
5. He (took/has taken) tennis lessons since 2010.
6. She (woke up/has woken up) early today.

3) Conversation Activity — Have You Ever…?

Task *Look at the activities below and finish the "Have you ever…" questions in the blanks. Write one question of your own in the space at the bottom. Walk around the classroom and ask your classmates these questions. If someone answers "Yes," write down their name and then ask them, "How was that?" Then ask one more follow-up question you make up. Write the answers in the blanks.*

Example

A) Hi, Akiko. Have you ever traveled abroad?
B) Yes, I have. I went to Hawaii with my parents.
A) How was it?
B) It was a lot of fun.
A) Did you go to any beaches? ◄········ **Follow-Up Question**
B) Yeah, I went to Sunset Beach on Oahu. It was beautiful.

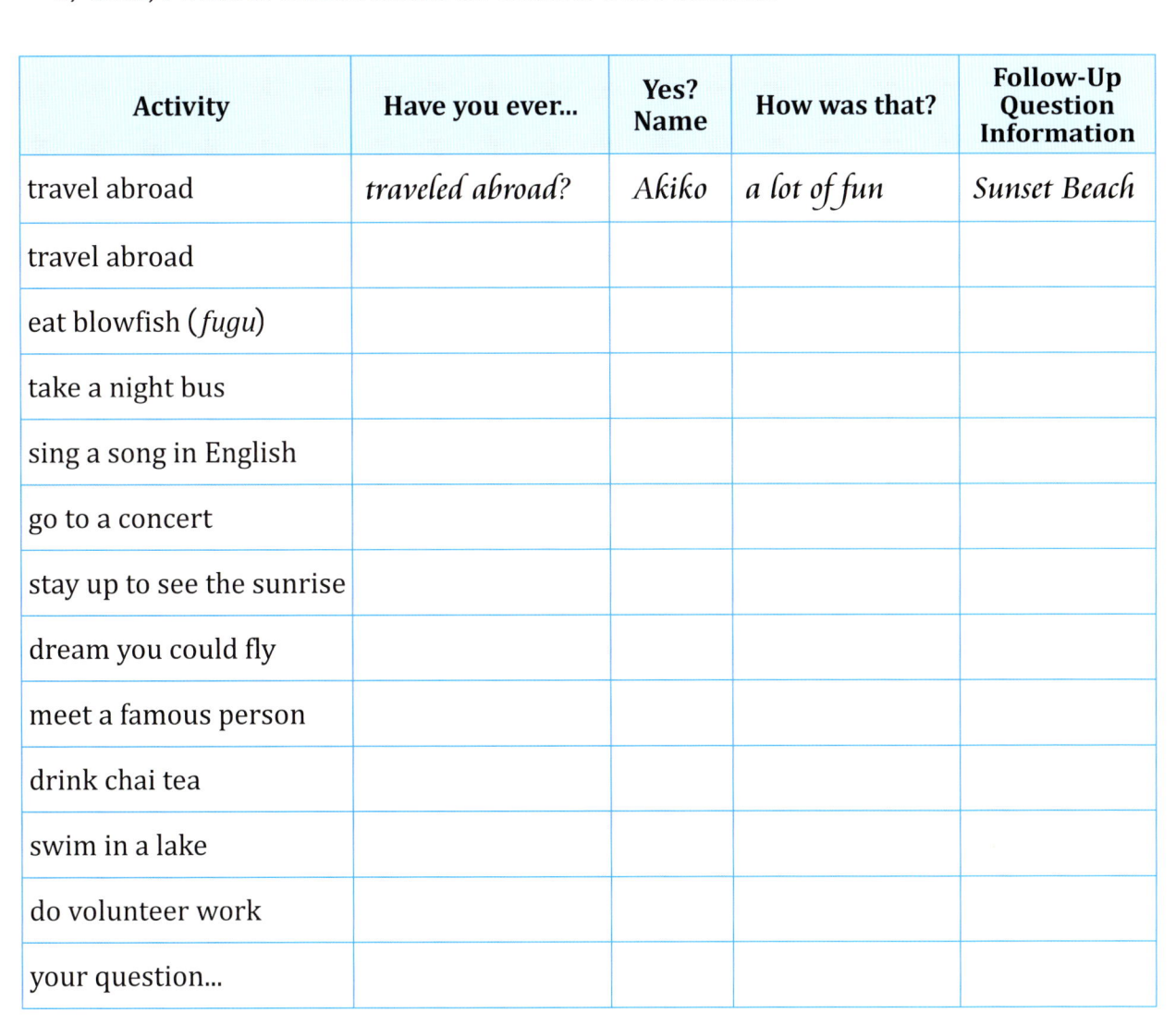

Activity	Have you ever…	Yes? Name	How was that?	Follow-Up Question Information
travel abroad	*traveled abroad?*	*Akiko*	*a lot of fun*	*Sunset Beach*
travel abroad				
eat blowfish (*fugu*)				
take a night bus				
sing a song in English				
go to a concert				
stay up to see the sunrise				
dream you could fly				
meet a famous person				
drink chai tea				
swim in a lake				
do volunteer work				
your question…				

Unit 11 *Talking About Travel*

4) Listening — About Travel

Task *Listen to the following passage. Write the words you hear in the blanks.*

I'll tell you about some of the trips I have taken. I have 1 _____.

Last year 2 _____. That was really fun.

We 3 _____.

I also 4 _____. That was great.

I have 5 _____.

But I want to, so 6 _____.

5) Write and Talk — About Trips You Have Taken

Task *Write about yourself. You can use the passage above as a model. When you finish, close the book and talk about trips you have taken with a partner or small group.*

Unit 12

Talking About Hometowns

1) Model Conversation — Hometowns

Task 1 *Two students talk about their hometowns. Practice this conversation with a partner.*

A: Hi. Could you tell me a little about your hometown?

B: Sure. I'm from Tokushima in Shikoku. Have you heard of it?

A: Yeah, there's a big festival there in the summer, right?

B: That's right. The "Awa Odori" is held there for four days in August. Some people dance all day and all night. And there's also great surfing at Ikumi Beach.

A: Are there any special foods in Tokushima?

B: Yeah, Tokushima is famous for its "Naruto Seaweed." It's really tasty!

A: Wow... Tokushima is more interesting than my hometown. Are there any bad points about living there?

B: Well, the nightlife in Tokushima is not as exciting as Tokyo or Osaka.

Task 2 *The conversation continues. Write in the missing questions and then practice with a partner.*

B: How about you? Where did you grow up?

A: I grew up in Kameoka. It's a small city outside of Kyoto. The population is about 100,000 people.

B: _____? ◀······· Follow-Up Question

A: It's famous for the "Hozugawa Kudari," a boat ride down the Hozu River to Arashiyama. It's a lot of fun!

B: _____? ◀······· Follow-Up Question

A: I've done it more than 5 times.

B: I see... Are there any special foods grown in Kameoka?

A: Yeah. A lot of foods grown in Kameoka are used in traditional Japanese restaurants in Kyoto. For example - yams, daikon and matsutake mushrooms.

B: Oh, matsutake... I want to try those one day!

Follow-Up Question Starters		
What...?	Who...?	How...?
When...?	Why...?	Where...?
Which...?	Whose...?	Are you...?
Can you...?	Do you...?	Did you...?
How long...?	How much...?	How many...?
How often do you...?	Have you ever...?	

2) Useful Language — Comparative Adjectives 1

Task 1 *Make comparative adjectives out of the adjectives below. Make sure you understand their meanings. Remember - When using adjectives to compare two things you should:*

1) add "er" to the end of short one-syllable adjectives
     or
2) put "more" or "less" before most longer adjectives
3) be careful that some two-syllable adjectives use "er"

cold ___*er*___	interesting ___*more*___	big _____
traditional _____	small _____	boring _____
expensive _____	urban _____	rural _____
exciting _____	multicultural _____	warm _____
dangerous _____	crowded _____	humid _____
noisy _____	beautiful _____	quiet _____
hot _____	polluted _____	busy _____

Task 2 *Write three sentences of your own using the adjectives above to compare two cities that you know about.*

Examples - Tokyo is <u>bigger than</u> Nagoya.
  Kobe is <u>more multicultural than</u> Kumamoto.

1. _____
2. _____
3. _____

3) Useful Language — Comparative Adjectives 2

Task *We can also make comparative adjectives by using the "not as (adjective) as" pattern. Write three sentences of your own below comparing cities you know.*

Examples - Nagoya is <u>not as big as</u> Tokyo.
  Shizuoka is <u>not as exciting as</u> Osaka.
  Naha is <u>not as cold as</u> Sapporo.

1. _____
2. _____
3. _____

4) Conversation Activity — Guess the City Game

Task Make a group with two or three classmates. One member of your group thinks of a city. The other members try to guess the name of the city. The person answering the questions must use a sentence with a comparative adjective in it.

45

Example

A) I'm thinking of a city.
B) Is it Tokyo?
A) No, it's smaller than Tokyo.
C) Is it Nagoya?
A) No, it's more traditional than Nagoya.
D) Is it Kyoto?
A) No, it's not as big as Kyoto.
B) Is it Nara?
A) You're right! You got it.

Guess the City

Tokyo
Nara   Nagoya
Himeji   Osaka   Fukui
Fukuoka   Shizuoka   Hiroshima   Kobe
Sapporo   Chiba   Naha   Yokkaichi
Yokohama   Sendai   Kumamoto
Kawasaki   Niigata
Kyoto

Unit 12 Talking About Hometowns

5) Listening — Hometowns

Task *Listen to the following passage. Write the words you hear in the blanks.*

I'll tell you about my hometown. I grew up in 1_____ .

The population is about 2_____ . My hometown is well known for

 3_____ . Every year 4_____ there.

A lot of 5_____ are grown near my hometown. One bad point

about my hometown is that it's 6_____ .

6) Write and Talk — Your Hometown

Task *Write about yourself. You can use the passage above as a model. When you finish, close the book and talk about your hometown with a partner or small group.*

_____
_____
_____
_____
_____
_____
_____
_____
_____
_____
_____
_____

Unit 13

Talking About Your Opinions

1) Model Conversation — What Do You Think?

Task 1 *Three students talk. Practice this conversation with a partner.*

A: What do you think is the best kind of movie for a first date? Action, comedy, drama, suspense...?

B: Well, I think action movies are the best for a first date. They're the most exciting, so you both feel great afterwards.

A: Really? I think dramas are the best. A drama gives you something to talk about after the movie.

C: No way! Comedy movies are the best for a first date. They're the most fun. They make you laugh and put you in a good mood.

A: That's interesting. We're good friends but have very different opinions.

Task 2 *The conversation continues. Write in the missing questions and then practice with a partner.*

A: How about music? What music do you like to listen to when you study?

B: My favorite music is rock music. But I don't like to listen to rock when I study. The best music for me when I study is classical music.

C: Oh really? _____? ◀········ Follow-Up Question

B: My favorite composer is Beethoven.

A: Classical music? ...You're kidding! Beethoven would make me too sleepy. I need heavy metal music with the volume turned up loud. Then I can study all night long!

B: _____? ◀········ Follow-Up Question

A: No. My family never complains. I always wear earphones.

C: Well, I disagree with both of you. I need silence when I study. I just want my books, my computer and a cup of coffee. That's the best way for me to study.

Follow-Up Question Starters		
What...?	Who...?	How...?
When...?	Why...?	Where...?
Which...?	Whose...?	Are you...?
Can you...?	Do you...?	Did you...?
How long...?	How much...?	How many...?
How often do you...?	Have you ever...?	

2) Useful Language 1 — Superlatives in Facts and Opinions

Task *We use superlatives to give facts and opinions. Write three statements using superlative adjectives below. Remember - Superlative adjectives are made a lot like comparative adjectives.*

1) add "est" to the end of short one-syllable adjectives (big = the biggest)
2) put "most" or "least" before longer adjectives (exciting = the most exciting)
3) be careful that some two-syllable adjectives use "est"

Examples - Lake Biwa is the biggest lake in Japan.
New York is the most exciting city to live in.

1. _____
2. _____
3. _____
4. _____
5. _____

3) Useful Language 2 — Agreeing and Disagreeing

Task *Here are some ways to give your opinion, and agree and disagree in English. Use these expressions to agree or disagree with the statements below.*

Opinion Markers	Agree	Disagree
I think... I feel that...	I agree.	Really? I don't agree.
In my opinion...	I think so too.	No, I don't think so.
If you ask me....	That's true.	Sorry, I disagree.
	Yeah. You're right!	You're kidding!
		No way!

1. I think salmon is the most delicious fish.

   Agree or Disagree? _____

2. In my opinion baseball is the most exciting sport.

   Agree or Disagree? _____

3. If you ask me, Osaka is the most interesting city to live in.

   Agree or Disagree? _____

4) Conversation Activity — Giving Your Opinion

Task *Fill in the blanks to make your opinions. Add two of your own opinions in the boxes at the bottom. Work with a partner or small group and take turns telling your opinions. People should agree or disagree with you and tell their opinions. Be sure to start with an opinion marker. Then write a ○ in the box to show if people agree or disagree with you. Ask follow-up questions to continue the conversation.*

Example

A) I think watermelon is the most delicious fruit.
B) I don't agree. In my opinion strawberries are the most delicious.
A) What other fruits do you like?
B) I really like mango.

Opinion	Agree	Disagree	Follow-Up Information
_____ is the most delicious fruit.			
_____ is the cutest animal.			
_____ movies are the best kind of movie for a first date.			
_____ is the most fashionable brand of clothing			
_____ is the funniest comedian.			
_____ is the most serious environmental problem.			
_____ is the most exciting sport.			
_____ is the best music for studying.			
_____ is the most interesting TV show.			
_____ is the most entertaining computer game.			
_____ is the best season for romance.			
(your opinion)			
(your opinion)			

5) Listening — Opinions

Task *Listen to the following passage. Write the words you hear in the blanks.*

I'll tell you a few of my opinions. I think 1 _____ .

Do you agree? In my opinion 2 _____ .

I feel that 3 _____ . Also, I think

 4 _____ .

And you may think I'm crazy but I don't think 5 _____ .

And here's one more opinion... If you ask me, 6 _____ .

6) Write and Talk — About Your Opinions

Task *Write about yourself. You can use the passage above as a model. When you finish, close the book and talk about your opinions with a partner or small group.*

_____
_____
_____
_____
_____
_____
_____
_____
_____
_____
_____

Unit 14

Talking About Future Plans

1) Model Conversation — What Are Your Plans?

Task 1 *Two students talk about their plans. Practice this conversation with a partner.*

A: Hi, what are you going to do this evening?

B: Well, I'll probably just go home and take it easy tonight. How about you?

A: After dinner I will go to the gym and work out a bit. I'll finish around 9. Maybe I'm going to meet a friend after that for coffee.

B: How about tomorrow? Do you have any plans?

A: No, not really. My sister is in the Dance club at her university, and they will do a show tomorrow night. I'm probably going to go.

B: That sounds fun. I'd like to join you but I have to study for a test.

Task 2 *The conversation continues. Write in the missing questions and then practice with a partner.*

B: Do you have any plans for the vacation?

A: Maybe I'll buy a new computer. I will probably read a lot. Definitely, I'm going to look for a new part-time job.

B: _____? ◀······· **Follow-Up Question**

A: I don't like the job I have now. I can't stand my boss, the pay is low and sometimes I have to work until late at night.

B: _____? ◀······· **Follow-Up Question**

A: I'll probably look for a restaurant job. I like to work with people, and usually you can finish by 10 at night. How about you? What are your plans for the vacation?

B: I'm not sure what I'll do. But I'll graduate next year, so definitely I'm going to have some fun this vacation!

Follow-Up Question Starters

What...?	Who...?	How...?
When...?	Why...?	Where...?
Which...?	Whose...?	Are you...?
Can you...?	Do you...?	Did you...?
How long...?	How much...?	How many...?
How often do you...?	Have you ever...?	

2) Useful Language — Adverbs of Probability

Task 1 *Here are some expressions we use when we talk about the future. Practice the sentences and notice the likelihood they are used to express.*

Adverb of Probability	How Likely?	Examples
×	100%	I will(I'll)... eat soba for lunch today. I'm going to...
Definitely	100% (with emphasis)	I will(I'll) <u>definitely</u>... go to bed early tonight. <u>Definitely</u>, I will(I'll)... I'm <u>definitely</u> going to... <u>Definitely</u>, I'm going to...
Probably	60-99%	I will(I'll) <u>probably</u>... meet a friend tomorrow. <u>Probably</u>, I will(I'll)... I'm <u>probably</u> going to... <u>Probably</u>, I'm going to...
Maybe	5%-60%	<u>Maybe</u> I will(I'll)... take a trip abroad this winter. <u>Maybe</u> I'm going to...

Task 2 *Think about the future and complete the sentences below using the expressions in the box above. Join a group of 3 or 4 and share your answers.*

Examples

    After class I'll probably study in the library.
               or
    After class I'm probably going to study in the library.

1. After class... _____

2. Tonight... _____

3. Tomorrow... _____

4. This weekend... _____

5. During the next vacation... _____

6. After I graduate... _____

3) Conversation Activity — Vacation Plans

Task *First, complete the three sentences below about your plans for the next vacation. Then walk around the classroom and talk with your classmates about their plans. Write the information in the blanks. Do sure to ask follow-up questions and write that information in the blanks.*

Definitely - _____

Probably - _____

Maybe - _____

Example

A) Hi, Hiroko. What are your plans for the next vacation?

B) Well, I'm definitely going to work at my part-time job.
I'll probably go to a hot spring with my mother and sister.
And maybe I'll take a trip to Guam.

A) I see. What hot spring will you go to? ◀······ **Follow-Up Question**

B) We'll probably go to Arima Hot Springs near Kobe.

Name	Definitely	Probably	Maybe	Follow-Up Information
Hiroko	part-time job	hot springs	Guam	Arima Onsen

4) Listening — Vacation Plans

Task *Listen to the following passage. Write the words you hear in the blanks.*

I'll tell you about my plans for the vacation. I will definitely 1 _____

_____ . I'm going to 2 _____ ,

and 3 _____ . Maybe 4 _____ .

Probably, 5 _____ .

I really want to have a fun vacation because next year 6 _____

_____ .

5) Write and Talk — About Your Plans for the Vacation

Task *Write about yourself. You can use the passage above as a model. When you finish, close the book and talk about your plans for the vacation with a partner or small group.*

- 68 -

Review and Reflection — Units 10-14

Task *Use the questions below to help you review and reflect on what you have studied in the last five units.*

1. What new words, expressions, or grammar patterns did you learn and think are important to remember?

   _____
   _____
   _____
   _____
   _____

2. Write sentences using these new words, expressions or grammar patterns.

   _____
   _____
   _____
   _____
   _____
   _____
   _____

3. What else did you learn about language, culture or language learning?

   _____
   _____
   _____
   _____

Unit 15
Review and Practice

1) Review — Conversation Game

Task This game will help you practice the language you have learned in this textbook. To play the game, form a small group and follow the directions.

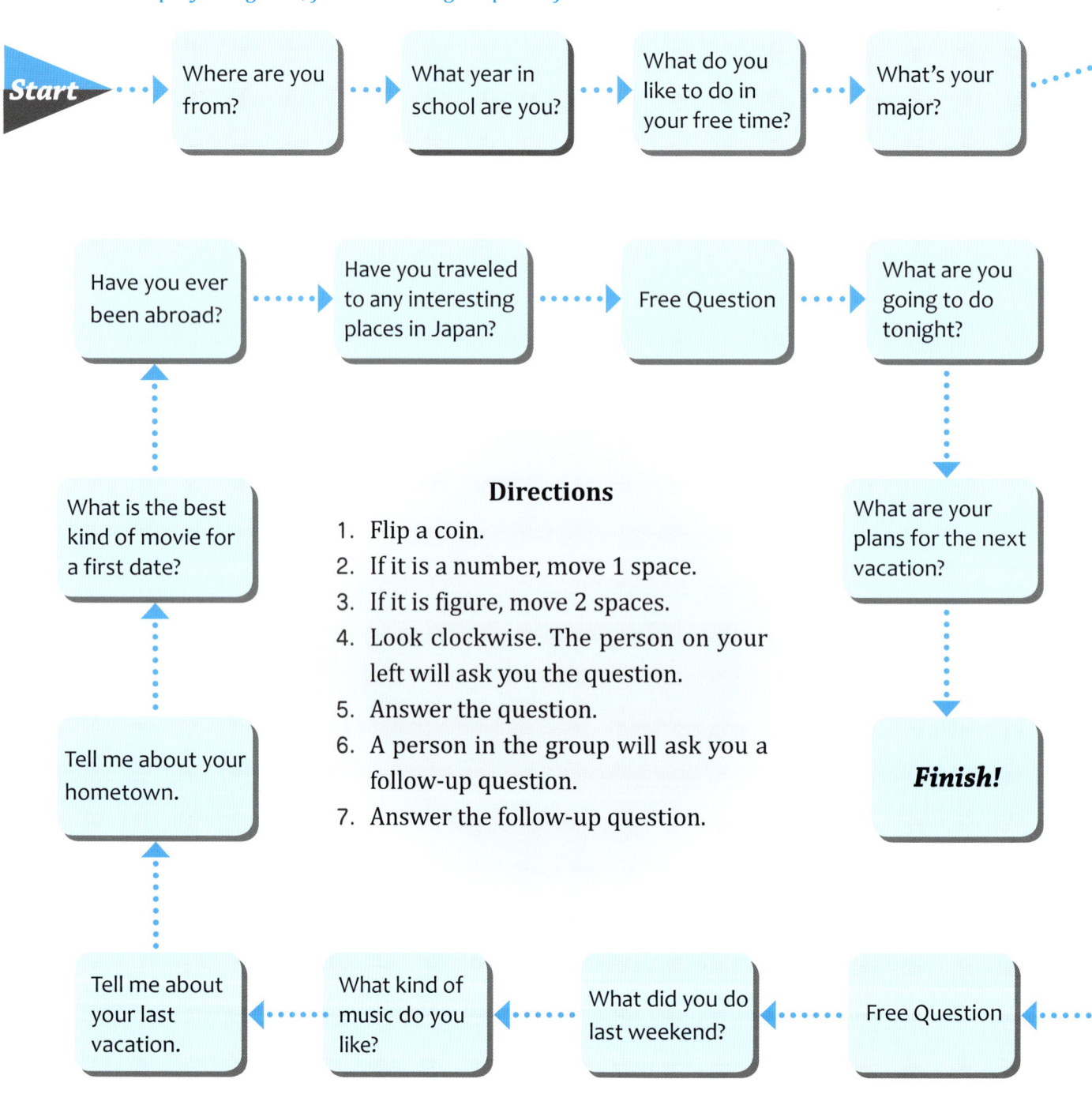

Start → Where are you from? → What year in school are you? → What do you like to do in your free time? → What's your major? →

Have you ever been abroad? → Have you traveled to any interesting places in Japan? → Free Question → What are you going to do tonight? → What are your plans for the next vacation? → **Finish!**

What is the best kind of movie for a first date?

Tell me about your hometown.

Tell me about your last vacation. → What kind of music do you like? → What did you do last weekend? → Free Question →

Directions

1. Flip a coin.
2. If it is a number, move 1 space.
3. If it is figure, move 2 spaces.
4. Look clockwise. The person on your left will ask you the question.
5. Answer the question.
6. A person in the group will ask you a follow-up question.
7. Answer the follow-up question.

What's your favorite class? → Do you live alone or with your family? → Tell me about your typical day. → Free Question

↓

How do you come to school?

↓

How often do you skip breakfast?

↓

Tell me about your family. (How many?)

↓

How often do you study on the weekend?

↓

Tell me the recipe for a dish you can cook. ← What foods do you like? ← Tell me about a family member. (Appearance) ← Tell me about a friend. (Personality)

Follow-Up Question Starters

What…?	Who…?	How…?
When…?	Why…?	Where…?
Which…?	Whose…?	Are you…?
Can you…?	Do you…?	Did you…?
How long…?	How much…?	How many…?
How often do you…?	Have you ever…?	

Unit 15 *Review and Practice*

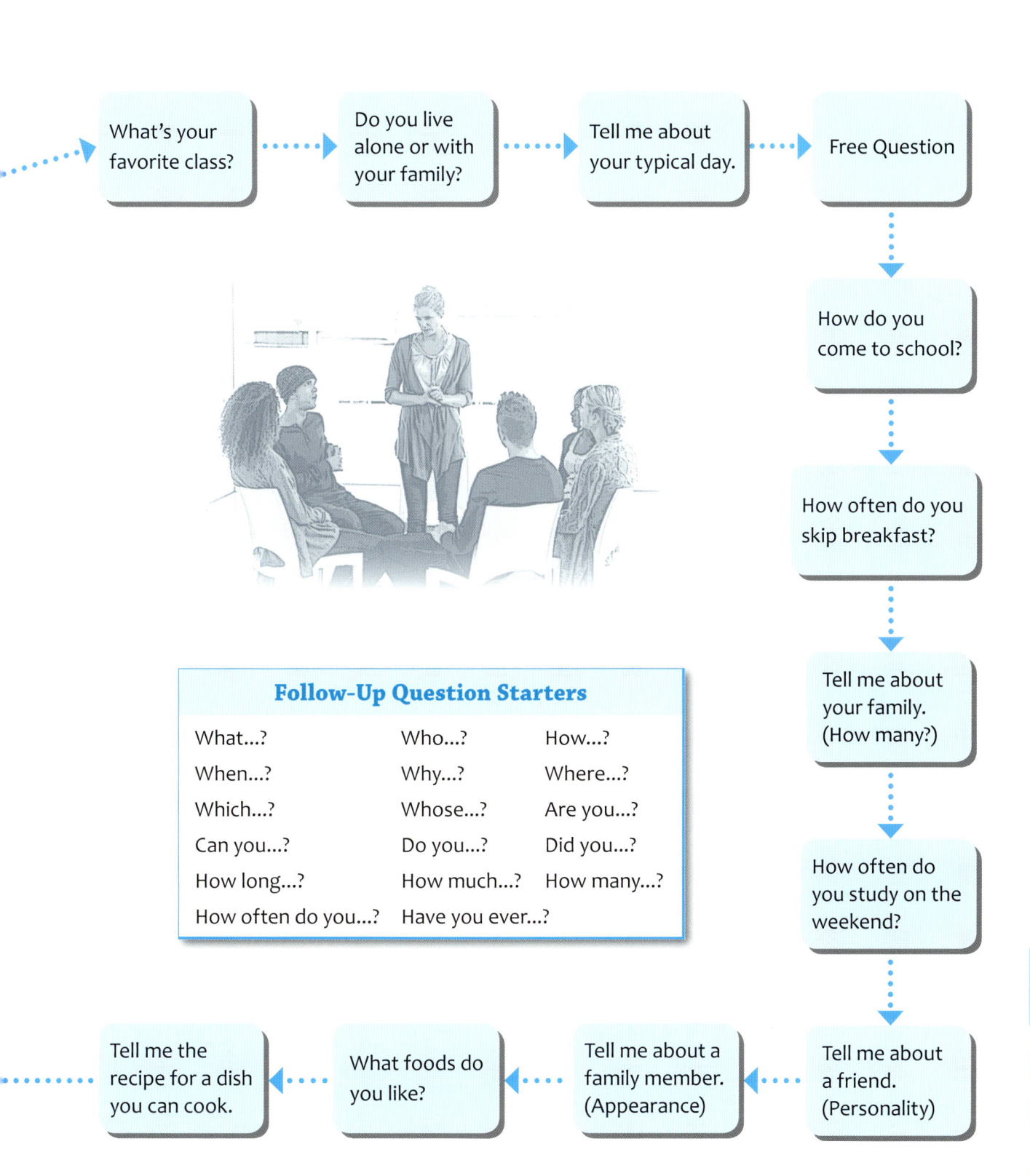

- 71 -

2) Review — Conversation Management Expressions

Task *Read these short dialogues and write the expression from the box below that best fits the conversation.*

1) A: What did you do over the vacation?
   B: _____.
   A: Sure. What did you do over the vacation? You know...did you go anywhere?
   B: Yeah, I went to my grandparent's house.
   A: I see.

2) A: One of my favorite Japanese words is "なんとなく."
   B: _____.
   A: In English I guess we would say, "one way or another."

3) A: Can you tell me the population of Nagoya?
   B: _____.
   A: OK. I will check it out on the internet.

4) A: How did you like your homestay in America?
   B: It was OK but my homestay mother always said I was "disorganized."
   A: _____.
   B: In Japan we would say I'm "しまえない." (整理整頓ができない)

5) A: _____.
   B: Yes, how can I help you?
   A: Please tell me about today's homework.

6) A: Can I ask you a question?
   B: Sure.
   A: _____.
   B: It's spelled, I-M-A-G-I-N-A-T-I-O-N.

7) A: There is a TV program I really want to see tonight.
   B: _____. What is it?
   A: It's a program about the Olympics.

Conversational Expressions	
How do you spell that word?	Could you repeat that please?
I see.	Sorry, I don't know.
What's the Japanese word for that?	Excuse me.
How do you pronounce this word?	How do you say that in English?

3) Review — Follow-Up Questions

Task *Pretend you are in a conversation and your friend makes these statements. Write Follow-Up Questions for each statement.*

1) A: I really like playing computer games.
   B: _____?
   A: My favorite game these days is Street Fighter.

2) A: Tomorrow I will play some tennis.
   B: _____?
   A: I will play with my friend Bill.

3) A: I bought a new pair of shoes yesterday.
   B: _____?
   A: They cost about 7,000 yen.

4) A: I want to go to Europe next year.
   B: _____?
   A: I want to go to France and Spain.

5) A: I have a big family.
   B: _____?
   A: There are six people in my family.

4) Review — Important Vocabulary

Task *Match the word or phrase on the left with the word or phrase on the right that is closest in meaning. Put the letter in the space. The first one has been done for you.*

1. major   _g_
2. hard   ____
3. funny   ____
4. beard   ____
5. a couple of times   ____
6. cheap   ____
7. eggplant   ____
8. urban   ____
9. No way!   ____
10. really   ____

a. disagree
b. not expensive
c. twice
d. purple vegetable
e. in the city
f. hair all over the face
g. main subject of study
h. very
i. makes people laugh
j. difficult

Extra Activities

1) Conversation Activity — Guess About Your Classmate

Task *Sit next to someone you don't know very well and follow these steps.*

1. Write the questions in the blank.
2. Guess what your partner's answers might be for each question.
3. Ask your partner the questions and write the answers in the blank.
4. Ask follow-up questions and write these answers in the blanks.

Information	Question	Your Guess	Partner's Answer	Follow-Up Question Answers
First name (not family name)	*What's your first name?*			
Hometown				
Hobby				
Favorite color				
Favorite season				
Birth month				
Favorite sport to watch				
Part-time job				
Favorite food				
Food he/she doesn't like				
Favorite TV show				
Favorite band or singer				
Singer or TV star he/she doesn't like				
Your question...				

How many times did you guess correctly? _____

2) Conversation Activity — Find Someone Who... (After New Years)

Task Look at the question topics under "Find someone who..." and write questions in the blanks. Also make up two Yes/No questions of your own. Go around the class and ask your classmates the questions. When someone answers "Yes," write their name in the blank. Be sure to ask follow-up questions and write that information in the blank too.

Find someone who...	Question	Name	Follow-Up Question Answers
...worshipped at a shrine on New Year's Day	*Did you worship...*		
...rang a temple bell on New Year's Eve			
...went snowboarding			
...took a trip to an onsen			
...gave a New Year's gift (otoshidama)			
...ate sweet black beans (kuromame)			
...had a romantic Christmas Eve			
...went to a grandparent's house			
...bought a lucky bag (fukubukuro)			
...had a good dream New Year's morning			
...saw the sun rise on January 1st			
...flew a kite			
...will have very good luck this year (daikichi)			
your question			
your question			

3) Conversation Activity — Giving Clear Directions

Task *This activity gives you practice with the words and phrases used to give good, clear directions. Follow these steps:*

1. Leave the classroom with a partner or small group and hide an object somewhere on campus.
2. While you are walking, write down directions on how to find the object.
3. When you get back to class, write clear directions on a piece of paper.
4. Exchange your directions with another group of students. Follow their directions to find the object they have hidden outside.

Model Directions

First, go out the door and turn right/left.

Next, walk down the hall and go down the stairs.

Then, go out of the building and turn right.

After that, walk straight until you come to   the cafeteria.
　　　　　　　　　　　　　　　　　　　　　　　　Building 3.
　　　　　　　　　　　　　　　　　　　　　　　　the parking lot.
　　　　　　　　　　　　　　　　　　　　　　　　the athletic field.
　　　　　　　　　　　　　　　　　　　　　　　　the library.
　　　　　　　　　　　　　　　　　　　　　　　　the big tree.

Finally, you will find the pen   next to the tree.
　　　　　　　　　　　　　　　　　　on top of the bush.
　　　　　　　　　　　　　　　　　　under the trash can.
　　　　　　　　　　　　　　　　　　in the corner.
　　　　　　　　　　　　　　　　　　in back of the sign.

Remember:

1) Don't leave anything valuable behind.
2) Always stay with your group.
3) Come right back to class. Don't get lost!

Notes:

_____

_____

_____

4) Language Learning Strategy — New Word Cards

Task *When learning a language it's important to build your vocabulary as quickly as possible. Repeated exposure to a word is a key to remembering the word, but if you wait for the word to show up in a conversation or in what you read or a movie or music, it can take a long time to learn the word. A good way to speed up this process is to use word cards. Word cards are great because they can be used as often as you like, and at times you find convenient, on the bus, train etc. Here is what they look like:*

Example

(uncountable noun)
○ Spinach
Last night I ate spinach for dinner.

○ほうれん草
昨日の夕食でほうれん草を食べた。

Directions:

1) Choose words or expressions you think are important to remember from your lesson, a book, movie or music you are listening to.

2) Write the word or expression on one side of the word card in English. On the other side write the word or expression in Japanese. Write the part of speech of the word above the word in English.

3) Below the word write the word or expression in a short sentence. On the other side of the card write the sentence translated into Japanese.

4) Every day look at your word card collection. Look at the English word or expression and try to remember what it means. Check the Japanese side of the card to see if you remembered correctly. You can also look at the Japanese word first and see if you remember the English.

5) When you remember the word correctly for three days in a row, put the word card into a separate ring for words you have learned. Review this ring of word cards every week or so, and if you can't remember the meaning of the word, put it back into the ring of words you want to learn.

Eric Bray

www.ericbray.com

For further English practice,
use the website found at:

http://www.ericbray.com/eric-brays-english-study-resource-online

Eric Bray's English Study Resources Online

Listening

Pronunciation

Reading

Chat Opportunities

Grammar

Culture

Dictionaries

Quizzes and Games

Feedback

Image Credit:
©360b / Shutterstock.com: p43
イラスト：
©gatta nera（銀月堂）: p30, p31

著作権法上、無断複写・複製は禁じられています。

New Time to Communicate	[B-791]
コミュニケーション初級英語講座［改訂新版］	

1 刷	2015 年 2 月 23 日
12 刷	2025 年 3 月 21 日

著 者	エリック・ブレイ　　　Eric Bray
発行者	南雲　一範　　Kazunori Nagumo
発行所	株式会社　南雲堂 〒 162-0801　東京都新宿区山吹町 361 NAN'UN-DO CO., Ltd. 361 Yamabuki-cho, Shinjuku-ku, Tokyo 162-0801, Japan 振替口座：00160-0-46863 TEL：03-3268-2311（代表）／FAX：03-3269-2486 編集者　加藤　敦
組　版	柴崎　利恵
装　丁	銀月堂
検　印	省略
コード	ISBN978-4-523-17791-3　　C0082

Printed in Japan

E-mail　　nanundo@post.email.ne.jp
URL　　　https://www.nanun-do.co.jp/